Out of the Fire

A Mystical Exploration
of the
Ten Commandments

Out of the Fire

A Mystical Exploration
of the
Ten Commandments

C. Suzanne Deakins

One Spirit Press
Portland, Oregon

ISBN: 978-1-893075-72-6
LCCN: 2011906017

Spirit Press
Little Book Series

Making Spiritual Truth a
common force for the good of all.

Permissions to reprint and use in any manner other than
journal review must be obtained from

One Spirit Press

Portland, Oregon
www.onespiritpress.com

Introduction

Understanding the paradigm of our humanity is a key step in unlocking our relationship with the creator source, our divinity. Until we understand what we carry in our collective unconscious mind, we cannot fully embrace our spiritual life and relationship with God and Truth. The sojourn in this life is not about escaping our life but rather embracing our humanity and the relationship with God. The Ten Commandments are guides for understanding the connection to Truth and God.

For a long time we have looked at the Ten Commandments as rules and laws governing the better good of humankind. Most of us pay little attention to their importance. With apparent greed and lack of ethical and moral grounding throughout the globe, we are forced to look again at these laws. The Ten Commandments are the guideposts for the journey we take. Here we are given the help and natural spiritual laws that rule the spiritual community of life.

Spiritual laws are basic to the nature of reality. They are not man-made rules meant to benefit a certain or specific group of people or to regulate behavior. A spiritual law is like mathematics. The law of mathematics remains constant no matter what the circumstances. It is impersonal, yet sets the path for understanding. 3+3=6 remains so no matter where you are on earth.

So like physical law and mathematics once we grasp the underlying paradigm (laws) of our spiritual nature we become spiritual physicists. Many things become possible that only seem a far off dream and fantasy. When you understand the law of mathematics many things can occur... great music can be written... or check books balanced...or discoveries of our universe. And so it is with understanding spiritual law. Great intimacy of spirit can be shared with our brothers and sisters on this journey and the relationship with our creator becomes profound in unfathomable ways.

The Bible and Torah as well as other spiritual and religious works give us a glimpse into the collective unconscious of our species. There is no argument about them being fact at this point in history. Fact, true or not is of little concern as they are archetypical and play a major role in how consciousness unfolds in our life. These works gives steps and ways of freeing ourselves from the fascination with the illusions and delusions we live with daily. They point the way and give paths whereby we can return to our source our divinity.

Through the centuries of existence on this planet, we have become addicted to a misinterpretation of our senses. We believe rather than know. To return to our spiritual path we must become the knower... the Gnostic.

These works give us instructions perhaps into our DNA. Many times I have found myself experiencing the symbols represented by the role players in the Bible. To dismiss the religious writings of the past as of no consequence is similar to ignoring the need for water and air. They are an important part of our DNA structure and probably as important to our well being as water and air.

As I researched and read what others had written about the 10 Commandments, I became aware these were not just laws for better human good. But, in fact, are laws, and rules, such as a math or physics principles that govern the very way we live our spiritual lives. I did not fully comprehend what was presented until I reached the 10th Commandment, Thou Shall Not Covet. As I worked on this Commandment I began to understand more deeply the real journey we are on.

All of the Commandments show us the steps necessary to return to our source. We long to return to the origin of our divinity. In our unconscious mind it is this drive to return to the causer of life. I hear others talk of it as if it were a longing to leave this planet and return to their place of origin. How ever you feel it, see it, and long for it, it is the same. A longing to return to a state of pure energy, of consciousness aware of consciousness, of knowing we are one with the creator source. The creator source can be called God or Truth by many different languages, but it is the same. It is the source of our creation of our being.

Our spiritual journey begins when we realize we are and we exist, I AM. Our next step is negotiating the business of I AM and how are we to use this knowledge in our day-to-day interactions. Finally we must reach the collective state of We Are the infinite variety of consciousness unfolding as one energy, idea, and existence. This is not a mushy oneness where we our identity is lost. In fact, this state increases our identity not as a human but as a spiritual being creating our world. As we merge or free our billions of neurons into the collective neurons of the universe, we experience the thrill of finding our true family.

The excitement of knowing our identity fills us with electrical impulses that push us further into the realms of consciousness.

Simply put the Ten Commandments are the guidelines that help you reach this indescribable state of bliss.

The Ten Commandments, as I have written about them, are stated in Ontological terms. I have used the older translations of the Western Bible and other religious works to help in understanding and interpretation.

C. Suzanne Deakins

West Linn, Oregon
June 2011

Mystical Exploration of the Ten Commandments

"It is not that we keep His commandments first, and that then He loves; but that He loves us, and then we keep His commandments. This is that grace, which is revealed to the humble, but hidden from the proud..." - Augustine

Beginnings

God speaks to Moses on the mountain out of the fire. There is no voice coming from the clouds, stones, or earth, but from the fire God speaks. Stepping into this place of fire that does not consume but burns everlasting we are given the rules, laws, and covenants for a community of spiritual beings experimenting with humanity. The Ten Commandments are the archetypes for the rules we must follow if we are to go on this spiritual journey to the Promised Land, the land of milk and honey, and heaven. Just as there are laws (rules) that govern math so are there rules about our spiritual life and journey. The laws point to the direction we must take as we free ourselves from the illusion and dream state of consciousness.

The fire feels almost minor to the Ten Commandments but is central to understanding their importance and the archetypes they represent. An experience of God and Truth is not an intellectual endeavor but rather a creative moment. The intellect cannot comprehend the vastness of infinity or eternity or the power represented by God and Truth. This type of experience is known for one great instant, setting off neurons exploding throughout our consciousness, causing a great cascade of pleasure that changes the very nature of reality in our experience. Through this experience of fire, this firing of neurons and the explosion of pleasure we experience God and Truth. The stone tablet, the clouds, or any other object, don't speak as God and Truth.

God is known and speaks through the fire. Perhaps in the flash of orgasm when all sense of self is diminished to this fire is a knowing of God. The fire is an archetype symbol of the creative nature that is never consumed. The fire is the eternal androgynous self, the living male/female being carried within our consciousness.

Mystical Exploration of the Ten Commandments

*I am the Lord your God who brought you out of
the land of Egypt and the house of slavery. You
shall have no other gods before me.*

The First Commandment
You shall have no other gods before me.

Out of the fire God says: *I am the Lord your God who brought you out of the land of Egypt and the house of slavery. You shall have no other gods before me.* The First Commandment is implicit in the course of action we must take as spirit participating in a spiritual community. It does not deny there are other gods, nor make any claim of monotheism. It says this self is in the fire. It is this creative nature that speaks to us.

The power (God) of creativity releases us from the land of thinking material and physical being is all there is. We are released from this illusion and false sense of homeland. This illusion, this state of consciousness is represented by Egypt. The pharaoh is the king or overlord of this state of consciousness. House is the archetype of *state of being.* From the house of *slavery* says God, we are limited and slaves to this state of solid physical existence. Only when we use our creative energy can we be freed of this state of consciousness into Heaven.

From the center of consciousness, as fire, we experience that which is whole, complete, and perfect. Out of this state or place of consciousness we learn the *laws of*

7

our spiritual journey we must take to reach the Promised Land.

And God says this is what I have done...this is your story and freedom march. This source of power we call God/ Truth is saying I am more powerful, and above all other powers (gods) for I have the ability to free you from the enslavement of seeing life as physical, solid, and immutable. Thus you shall have no power higher, above me, or before me.

The word Lord actually has the antediluvian meaning of one before. Out of the fire God is saying I am the one great power that comes before all other power. In our spiritual journey we quickly learn our intention must be centered on this creative force. We learn neither magic nor beseeching will get us to the place we seek. No power or force other than this Lord, God and Truth will deliver us from our enslavement. Until this is understood no journey can be taken to the Promised Land. The promise, if we hear this commandment, is life eternal. Each day of our journey must begin by remembering this story of our freedom and who is responsible for it. There maybe other powers (gods) in your life but only the power that goes before (Truth) is capable of freeing you.

It is through remembrance we locate our direction in the journey. If you look at a map and don't know where you are, how can you find the direction you must take? In remembering our story, remembering the one who went before, we can set our compasses not on the illusion of the senses but on the fires of the creative force we carry within our consciousness.

When the beginning thought is on the axiomatic concept of the nature of reality then our working paradigm (conclusions) will be equal in nature and we will be freed of the slavery of misunderstanding the nature or reality, Truth. It is the misunderstanding that causes slavery. It is putting our attention on false or less powerful gods such as the pharaoh that keeps us slaves. In the story of Joseph we learn that our misinterpretation of life, of the dreams we live sells us into slavery and Egypt. Only when Joseph sees rightly, and interprets the illusions/dreams for what they are is he truly freed from his prison.

From the fire that never consumes we know we must remember how we sold ourselves into slavery by misunderstanding the illusion and dreams. Our starting point must be the nature of reality, the power that is called God and Truth.

Our divinity and relationship with the Creator Source is based on our spiritual sight. This is our ability to see beyond our beliefs to the nature of reality God, Truth and Absolute Love.

You shall not make for yourself an idol whether in the form of anything that is in the heaven above, or in the earth beneath or that is in the water under the earth. You shall not bow down to them or worship them.

The Second Commandment:
You shall not make for yourself an idol

You shall not make for yourself an idol whether in the form of anything that is in the heaven above, or in the earth beneath or that is in the water under the earth. You shall not bow down to them or worship them. This begins the oral tradition (preaching and teaching) and our seeking. We learn that no power or enlightenment is contained within an image. Only by understanding, hearing, (the word), and experiencing the one power (God and Truth) that brought us, brings us out of our enslavement. In the beginning was the word and the word was God(s).

Again we must understand what we see is like an oasis and holds no real power. It is the power of the word (meanings) we experience. We communicate what we know and understand through words. Our world is built out of words and the meanings we give them. By understanding we have the one power before all else (God) we can change the meaning and understanding for that which is more inclusive and intentionally set on the spiritual journey we take.

No image or single word can contain the vastness, the infinitude and ultimate power represented by the word God or Truth. Our journey is about the images and illusions we discard to reach the nature of reality, the conscious state of being conscious of consciousness. No image or worship (intentionalness) can make an image anything other than a symbol.

     This Second Commandment then says: by understanding the power and meaning in the word(s) can you know me (God and Truth); not in images or by sight but by understanding your world (consciousness) is built on words and the meanings you give them.

You shall not make wrongful use of the name of the Lord your God for the Lord will not acquit anyone who misuses his name.

The Third Commandment:
You shall not make wrongful use of the name of the Lord your God

You shall not make wrongful use of the name of the Lord your God for the Lord will not acquit anyone who misuses his name. We have learned that within the word we find the meaning and understanding of the journey we take. This Commandment means, literally, you shall not lift up or use the name in emptiness, without substance, in a trivial, worthless, or hollow manner. Name has the ancient meaning of nature. So the nature (name) of God shall not be used in this manner.

Prayer is the most common way we call upon the name of the Lord our God. Prayer and meditation both center our consciousness on the ultimate power of consciousness we call God and Truth. To pray for that which is trivial, or holds no real spiritual substance is to misuse the power found within the use of words. In prayer we begin to understand both the use of words and the reason the thoughts of God must be above and before all else.

Prayer centered on asking is praying amiss. We begin our prayer and meditation by centering our thinking on the thanksgiving of our deliverance from the house of slavery and Egypt. We acknowledge there is a power that can and will deliver us from this moment of slavery (pain, problem etc., is a spiritual slavery, ego mind). Before the problem the answer is... to solve our problem we must acknowledge the answer exists. 2+2=4 must have existence before the error, lack, or problem of 2+2=5 can appear.

We find ourselves in true worship by putting and acknowledging the answer (Truth/God, power) before all else. This means we don't bow down to the graven images. We are admonished not to use this power of creativity in vain or without true purpose of higher understanding. Commandments 1and 2 build to this moment and they (Commandments 1and 2) are the first steps bringing us to the beginning of our relationship with the concept of Truth/God. It is these steps JOB didn't understand. They are our story and they tell of our journey and beginning of freedom.

As in all worship we must surrender to the one source of our true freedom and power. In this surrender to purpose and being we find our selves enlightened and embraced by the nature of reality, Truth.

By remaining intentional to the nature of reality in our prayer and meditation we are fed the manna. Our very sustenance flows from our creative source. Wealth, health and all that we would ask to be restored unto us are seen as illusion and a misunderstanding of the one true power Truth.

This then tells us of the first steps of prayer, meditation, and translation. we must surrender to the Lord our God and give thanks for that which we have spiritually. Surrendering to the spiritual principle/law of all life allows us to experience our true divinity in an intimate relationship with God. All prayer, meditation and spiritual techniques are about building our relationship with God, understanding our divine nature and the true power of the fires we carry within.

We were/are created in love, absolute love and anything less is to miss-interpret our being and take the name of the Lord our God/Truth in vain.

Remember I am the Lord your God who
brought you out of the land of Egypt and the
house of slavery.

The Fourth Commandment:
Remember the Sabbath day, to keep it holy.

Remember the Sabbath day, to keep it holy. Six days shall thou labor, and do all thy work: But the seventh day is the Sabbath of the Lord thy God: in it thou shall not do any work, thou, nor thy son, nor thy daughter, thy manservant, nor thy maidservant, nor thy cattle, nor thy stranger that is within thy gates: For in six days the Lord made heaven and earth, the sea, and all that in them is, and rested the seventh day: wherefore the Lord blessed the Sabbath day, and hallowed it. Remember I am the Lord your God who brought you out of the land of Egypt and the house of slavery.

This is the commandment about surrender. It is common to end prayer with amen, or so it is. These are words that mean surrender. There are five phases on the path of Nirvana, The Promised Land, and Heaven. Five phases or steps if you will, in acquiring authentic forgiveness, and in manifesting consciousness in your life. At the end of these steps is the conclusion is always one of surrendering personal power (ego will) to a higher source. There is recognition you have done your spiritual work and acknowledging no matter the appearance or confusion there is a divine order at work. The sixth and seventh phases (steps) are the recognition (surrendering) to what is so about the nature of

God/Truth, all powerful creative force, and the acceptance of this is the day of rest or "so it is, amen."

Sabbath literally means a day of rest. It is a day of acceptance and intentional consciousness. The household, servants and beasts are all a description of your thoughts and states of awareness. In the older texts included the idea of slave, indicating in our unconscious mind in our thinking there are still thoughts that keep us in slavery and bound to Egypt and misunderstanding of the nature of reality. The work in this area must too rest or surrender to the higher force.

After our prayer (work), there must be a time of surrender, of rest. Honoring the Lord thy God is accomplished by knowing the ultimate power of life is the creative force. It goes beyond our ego and human understanding of life. We allow our work to be known and accept it as the one power before all else, Truth

On the sixth day God and Truth created life in its own image (humankind; male and female he created them.) The sixth day of our work is remembering all life is Truth manifesting in infinite variety. The androgynous nature of God and Truth is the ever living creative principle of male/female. No matter what the appearance it is all God and Truth. We give forth this unto the infinite eternal universe, and in doing so we surrender (the seventh day) all, allowing it to be.

In total surrender to God and Truth all thoughts, all ideas of our work, we give ourselves to that which has created us. We become one with the Divine nature of our being. We become intimate with God and Truth.

Honor thy father and mother, as the Lord thy God commanded you, so that your days may be long and it will go well with you in the land thy Lord your God is giving you.

The Fifth Commandment:
Honor thy father and mother.

Honor thy father and mother, as the Lord thy God commanded you, so that your days may be long and it will go well with you in the land thy Lord your God is giving you. This was not written to young children, so it has to have more meaning than obeying parents. This is a commandment about the androgynous nature of consciousness and relationships that form this state of being. It is about honoring the source of life and all creativity. Ultimately it is about honoring absolute love.

The feminine, mother, represents the spiritual nature of humanity and individuals. The Sophia stands on the top of the world with her arms outstretched accepting the wisdom and word of the divine. Archetypically Sophia, Ruth, wife, sister, all represent our spiritual nature.

The masculine represents physical being and reflections. Father/male the creator, God created the world. He created them male and female. In the new and old testaments of bible the concept of God is referred to as he. We see the masculine as the maker, progenitor, and planter of seeds. Sophia stands ready to receive the seeds of wisdom of God and Truth. In the new testament we see

Mary as the receptor of this wisdom as the seeds of God. These seeds manifests as the teaching of Jesus. Jesus brings a new interpretation of the Creator as one of absolute love. The teachings of Jesus are in many ways a different way of stating the older archetypes, an up-dating of the language.

The masculine hasn't any meaning without its' relationship to the feminine. For progeny the masculine must give of its wisdom and the feminine be willing to accept the wisdom. The feminine has no purpose without the acceptance of and relationship of male/wisdom. In spirit and body we are all male/female androgynous beings.

All creation and procreation takes male and female and only happens in an androgynous state awareness. To honor thy mother and father is to acknowledge creation. The word honor carries the ancient meaning of acknowledge. It is through the acknowledgment of our state of being we gain our spiritual heritage (land given to us by God). To honor our androgynous nature is to maintain the harmony and balance that is needed for the good of the spiritual community and our journey.

Honoring the mother and father is to praise the process that produces the Christ energy within, absolute love. The basis of all life is love. In our spiritual community it is love that binds us and in this we are one. In the name, nature, of Christ is the state of absolute love and acceptance of all life as consciousness.

Perhaps rather than not murder this
commandment should read.
Thou shall love, absolutely.

The Sixth Commandment:
Thou shall not murder.

The commandments are about keeping harmony and balance. These laws are to help us keep the natural flow of energy within consciousness, our spiritual community. All laws in the western hemisphere are weighed in this manner. The spirit of justice is about integrity, and maintaining the wholeness of our consciousness. Justice is not blind nor is it weighing the right and wrong. Justice seeks balance, harmony, and righteousness, right use of the creative forces we each carry within us.

The common definition of murder, used by many, is to kill. Throughout the Old Testament killing is specifically defined. Accidental death is not included in the concept of murder, neither is suicide nLor is unintentional killing. Murder in this commandment seems to be limited, and only includes intentional killing and pre thought or a plan of murder (premeditation).

Any intentional killing is upsetting to a community. The community feels vulnerable and out of balance and often reacts in fear. Intentional killing or murder is obviously not the right use of our creative energy. There are several places where laws about killing are given. In Numbers there is a lengthy explanation about absolute law allows no exceptions, no ifs, ands, or buts, and is very black and white in its application. Case law entertains the ifs, ands, buts when deciding fault. To fully understand this commandment and its use in our spiritual life we must go to the New Testament.

Keeping in mind that law is about maintaining the balance, harmony, and integrity of our consciousness, this commandment is not about actual physical murder. In the New Testament (Matthew 5:21-22) Jesus references this commandment. To paraphrase, he says to be angry without cause is to be liable to judgment. The attitude of hate and anger can lead to disruption in the flow of creative energy.

Nothing in consciousness is created outside of love. To have malice toward our brothers, reflections, thoughts is to disrupt the integrity and the wholeness of consciousness. When this happens we begin to have a lack of that which is whole, complete, and perfect appear in our perception. The harmony is disturbed. Hate, revenge, and malice are all misunderstandings of the nature of reality.

No problem, no pain or hurt has ever been solved or healed with hate and anger. The healing of our spiritual illness comes from love. Love without expectation. Love that embraces life comprehends by understanding the core or causer of our pain and anger, we can free ourselves of the slavery of misunderstanding.

For as long as we look at our brothers with anger, hate, and malice of forethought we will find ourselves judged and in the deepest prisons. Only by interpreting our consciousness, understanding the dream state of consciousness can we be free. We must embrace our brothers, thoughts and reflections, in absolute love. In love we free them as consciousness. In love we fulfill our cosmic intent. We are free to experience the integrity of consciousness conscious of consciousness.

Perhaps rather than thou shalt not murder this commandment should read, Thou shall love absolutely.

Thou Shall commit only absolute love
in holy trust

The Seventh Commandment:
Thou shall not commit adultery.

At the time the commandments were written there were many reasons to be strict about who slept with whom. The lines of inheritance were determined by the seed of the father so it was important to know who the father was. The way this commandment is presented steeps it in duality. Men, according to the Bible, were allowed to sleep with unmarried women, concubines and prostitutes. These acts did not constitute adultery. However, women were not allowed to have sex or intimate relations with anyone but their husband. It seems unreasonable and unfair this kind of law would be set down against women. Women were seen as property and therefore suffered under many laws of property, which the other commandments of not stealing and coveting seem to address.

Adultery is supposedly about infidelity, which is a trust issue in relationships. This commandment is like the rest of the commandments, it is about our spiritual life and community. Keep in mind it is important to maintain balance and integrity in the community. The word adultery is used throughout the bible in all kinds of circumstances, as well in the relationship of husband and wife. The etymology of the word adultery traces to such meanings as contamination, crossbreeding, corrupt, and debase, or make impure by the addition of a foreign or inferior substance or element. The word adultery is a Latin word. When used in the Roman language it acquires the idea of fixing or fastening to, which follows through with the idea of corruption via attaching or fixing a foreign element.

In the etymology of the word adultery we begin to see the reason for the commandment. This is about trying to mix magic with spiritual principle we call Truth. The union of husband and wife is about our spiritual union. In our spiritual union we find solace, purity of thought meaning our thoughts remain on God and Truth. All life and creation comes from the spiritual union. Only as our thoughts are centered on that which is so, God and Truth does life appear to us as whole, complete, and perfect.

From the very beginning of the commandments we are admonished to keep our spirituality, prayers, and worship centered only on God and this commandment is a repeat of this. If our prayers and thoughts are on producing magic or using magic, the illusion of a material and solid world, to produce what we feel we need in life we are contaminating the very idea of God and Truth.

When we try to use magic, illusion to accomplish our means we are saying there is more than God and Truth. In worship we honor our spiritual union with the idea of God and Truth. We must know as Job did that God is in every blade of grass and the furthest star, God and Truth are all there is. This lesson can be likened to 2+2=4 as God and Truth and then try to mix it with 2+2=5 an illusion/mistake/sin. The Truth, principle of the equation, is not hurt in any manner but our thought is contaminated and we don't see with purity of sight.

When this commandment tells us not to commit adultery we are being told to keep the bloodline pure. The life force represented by the bloodline must remain pure. It does no good to try to mix or contaminate it with thoughts that are not centered on God and Truth.

The union between husband and wife represents the spiritual union, a sacred trust. It is a trust given to us and accepted by us as one of love and acceptance of our spiritual nature. When we step outside of love or put conditions on love we are committing adultery, betraying the very core of our essence. In the Sermon on the Mount Jesus admonishes against the craving or lustful thoughts that cause adultery saying it begins in the heart. The heart is the center of love. If you lust or crave rather than love and honor the sacred trust of the union of the spirit that creates all life, you have committed adultery.

To hold the spiritual union in sacred trust in a place of absolute love is to know God and Truth. In this state our spiritual community sits in sanctified communion knowing love in the most sacrosanct way. Love produces all life.

Perhaps this commandment should read: Thou Shall commit only absolute love in holy trust

The man walked away very sad because he was wealthy. Jesus told His disciples: And again I say unto you, it is easier for a camel to go through the eye of a needle, than for a rich man to enter into the kingdom of God
(Mat. 19:21-24)

The Eighth Commandment:
Thou shall not steal.

To take another's belongings will of course disrupt the peace and harmony of any community. The implication is much more than the common idea of taking what is not ours. The seventh, eighth and tenth Commandments seem to be about possessions. Spiritually we have only our experience and absolute love. There aren't any possessions we must take on our journey. Ruth and Naomi find in their journey they must leave the possessions outside the city gate for they cannot take them through the eye of the needle, the needle's eye of the gate. This passage into the safety of the city allows only the person to enter and not their possessions. So to enter into a place of safe haven we must abandon our worldly possessions.

Again the idea of possessions come to mind: (Mat. 19:21) The man walked away very sad because he was wealthy. Jesus told His disciples, "And again I say unto you, it is easier for a camel to go through the eye of a needle, than for a rich man to enter into the kingdom of God"(Mat. 19:24).

The disciples were amazed at Jesus' statement and asked, "Who can be saved? Jesus then told them, With men this is impossible; but with God all things are possible" (Mat.

19:26). Possessions are not needed or wanted in the spiritual journey we take. Possessions don't secure a heavenly place. This commandment then, must refer to another concept rather than possessions.

The etymology of the word steal is the first clue and the root of it comes from ideas such as hide. It also carries a meaning of secret action. The word stealth has its origins in steal. But what are we not to hide? Thou shall not hide?

It appears most of the commandments refer back to the first Commandment of having no God before me. Each Commandment has reinforced the necessity of this central idea. The process of prayer and worship seems to maintain the focus of the one idea the one power, God/Truth, and ultimately absolute love. We know this is completely necessary if we are to align our thinking with Truth, the one power and one source. To enter into the second step of a syllogistic argument of all thought we must know that Truth is all there is or maintain our focus on the one idea, Truth. If this idea is hidden in the process there can be NO conclusion or alignment as Truth and we are left with an adulterated conclusion. We have already been warned of this in the seventh commandment. This seems like only part of this Commandment.

In the New Testament Jesus refers to the hidden aspect of spirituality. (Matthew 5: 14-16) 14 You are the light of the world. A city that is set on a hill cannot be hidden. 15 Nor do they light a lamp and put it under a basket, but on a lamp-stand, and it gives light to all who are in the house. 16 Let your light so shine before men, that they may see your good works and glorify your Father in heaven.

This doesn't mean you must go out and beat your chest and yell about your spiritual insights. It does, however, indicate that Truth is not to be hidden away like some dirty secret. Light suggests or is a symbol of knowledge and in the case of Jesus is, thought metaphysically, to be with the understanding of absolute love.

Throughout the New Testament Jesus tells us the acts committed in mind, in thought are no different than those we commit in physical life. He says adultery starts in the heart as does, anger and hate for our brothers. If this is so about our worldly thoughts then it is even more important for Truth, absolute love, God and Truth not to be hidden within our thoughts but in the forefront of our mind. Shinning the way for the path we are on.

Perhaps Thou shall not steal would be better understood as: Thou shall keep Truth and God and absolute love in the open and in the forefront of all thoughts.

Light gives of itself freely, filling all available space. It does not seek anything in return; it asks not whether you are friend or foe. It gives of itself and is not thereby diminished.

~*Michael Strassfeld*

The Ninth Commandment:
Thou shall not bear false witness

Most of us see this commandment as being the most useful in a court of law where we are summoned to bear witness in a legal proceeding. This commandment is indeed about not bearing false witness or lying. Lying is common in life. We tell the white lie to keep someone from being hurt, we tell a lie to keep from being entangled in an emotional-upheaval. There are cowardly lies, purposeful lies, and what some would call lies of acceptable good.

Acceptable lies seem to be those that protect a person. For instance, telling an abusive person his lover is not present when she is seems acceptable to most people. In human terms it is difficult to never lie. Lies are dependent on circumstances. Telling a deliberate falsehood against a neighbor is of course unsettling to any community. A community that is to live in harmony and balance must be one where lying and deceit are NOT a common way of communicating.

Of course, not bearing false witness means to tell the truth, but Truth in spiritual terms is not relative to changing circumstances. In John 8 Jesus says (to paraphrase) that NOT to speak or NOT do of God is to lie and when you lie, your Father or progenitor (causer) is the lie and it produces that which is around you.

In ontological terms this means the lie, the illusion, is producing the illusion, the false understanding or sin. What is at the foundation of our life is what we manifest and live out. Jesus says to the Rabbis were you the seed of Abraham you would do as Abraham. I am the seed of my Father and therefore can hear the words of my Father. You cannot hear the words because your very life is NOT of God, your Father. (again a paraphrase). Meaning Truth is known unto Truth. Ontological Truth or that which is so is not relative, it is all there is. To live other than by the very nature of God or all there is Truth, is to bear false witness. From the very beginning of the commandments we are admonished to keep the Lord Thy God in the forefront of our thoughts and life. And if this is not done then our Father or causer is not God but rather that which is nothingness, the devil.

Jesus said "But now, you are trying to kill me. You belong to your father the devil and you willingly carry out your father's desires. He was a murderer from the beginning and does not stand in the truth because there is no truth in him. When he tells a lie, he speaks in character, because he is a liar and the father of lies." (John 8:40-44)

Here Jesus indicates that to bear false witness is to try to kill that which is Truth or God. He admonishes us that before the laws and ways of Abraham, the Truth is, yes or before Abraham I AM. Truth exists before any lie or sin. It is the very foundation of our spiritual journey. We hear the meaning of Truth as Truth, not as the lie or sin. To live the Truth is to know the Lord Thy God leads us from the slavery of illusion and sin. To indicate in our words there is something outside of this is to bear false witness. By this we know the first thought, the major premise of all thought, must begin with the concept of God or Truth.

Once again Jesus tells those gathered to hear the words of God is to be set free and to live eternally and this can only be done with the understanding that we are the sons and daughters of God. God, Truth, and Consciousness are the causer or seed of all life. All life is infinite manifestation of God, Truth and Consciousness. Only if we live Truth do we have eternal life, understanding that *that which is so* is without beginning or end and is ever evenly eternally present.

Perhaps we should rewrite the 9th Commandment as Thou Shall live the Truth in words, as Consciousness.

Do not love the world or the things in the world. If anyone loves the world, the love of the Father is not in him. For all that is in the world--the <u>lust</u> of the flesh, the <u>lust</u> of the eyes, and the pride of life--is not of the Father but is of the world. And the world is passing away, and the lust of it; but he who does the will of God abides forever"

(1 John 2:15-17)

The Tenth Commandment:
Thou shall not covet.

Of all of the commandments this one perhaps carries the hardest task. Coveting deals with an underlying universal consciousness. The process of our creation seemingly separates us from our divine source. Although we seem to loose a certain amount of awareness of this divine source it is never fully erased from our consciousness. All life is a seeking to return to this source, to the divinity of our nature. Every act, no matter how convoluted, is an act of seeking our divinity and forming an intimate relationship with our understanding of God/Truth.

Our survival dynamics and attachment to the ego often keeps us from realizing this divinity we seek to know. Our intimacy with God and Truth can only occur when we allow the separated self to pass away. This is a mini death, an ego death. This occurrence allows us to experience state of oneness that expresses as totality, wholeness, and completeness. This event is one where we sense our perfection, not from a human point of view but from the perception of our divinity. Through life we seek out many substitutes for this experience, sex, love, money, knowledge, and fame. None of which give us the experience and wisdom of the Lord God and Truth.

Through life we learn to seek this unifying intimacy through many things. We start with our earliest experiences at the breast of our mother and later seek once again to satisfy, for a moment, our return to the creator source. When we are no longer at the breast we seek other things, more toys, more candy all in the search for the intimacy and peace we found in the womb. Freud was right, we desire to return to the source of creation. We desire to understand our creation as conscious beings.

Through life we collect many things. We seek to have more, to be more, looking for a substitute of our divinity and craving. We seek to know this unity and merging with the creator source. We become greedy thinking we can have more God and Truth by having more things. We see our neighbors and think they are happier than us. We think what we see is peace because they have found God and Truth and unity in their <u>things</u>. So, we crave the new car, we crave their things. We lust after what we feel is their pocket full of Truth and God. We become greedy and we covet our neighbor's wife. We covet their spirituality, thinking it will procure for us what we think we lack in life.

Only consciousness aware of consciousness can take you to that place of divinity and intimacy with God and Truth. No-thing exists that can satisfy this underlying hunger that drives our being so long and hard. No power can give you more God than your neighbor. Your neighbor's wife (meaning another's spirituality) is not yours to have. Like our thumbprint we must each form our individual relationship with God and Truth. We can't have more than our neighbor. No matter what the appearance your neighbor is not happier than you because they have found God in a new car or a powerful position.

The return to the creator source to understand our cosmic identity and divinity we must become aware of ego and the substitutes it tries to make for the ultimate epiphany of being intimate with Truth/God. The ego must die. It must pass into the nothingness of the illusion that we have ever been separate from our creator source. To reach this state of wisdom we learn not to be greedy, to stop the craving and lusting after another's understanding of the divine nature of being. We stop craving more things and we return to the simplicity and elegance of Truth and the Lord God. The beautiful wholeness, completeness and perfection are for us each to hold as our consciousness.

The universal consciousness is extremely powerful and we have had many generations of greed and trying to substitute our cosmic divinity with things of all sorts. The task of letting go of ego, greed, lusting, and craving is not an easy one, but through the practices of Truth and consciousness we can indeed have what our soul longs for, an intimate experience with God and Truth.

Perhaps the Tenth Commandment should read: Thou shall accept your divinity in all that is manifested in life.

Ontological Ten Commandments

The First Commandment: Know only that Truth is all there is. Keep Truth in the forefront of your thinking and thoughts. Our starting point must be the nature of reality, the power that is called God and Truth.

The Second Commandment: By understanding the power and meaning contained in the word(s) can you know me (God and Truth). Not in the images or by sight but by understanding that your world (consciousness) is built on words and the meanings you give them.

The Third Commandment: Thou shall surrender all idols and gods and appearances so you may know Truth and God. In doing so we experience the nature of reality or all there is, Truth. Surrendering the sense testimony you surrender to God and Truth and are intimate with the One.

The Fourth Commandment: Thou shall surrender all will and ego to the concept of Truth/God. We give forth our understanding of Truth unto the infinite eternal universe and in doing so we surrender (the seventh day) all, allowing it to be

The Fifth Commandment: We praise the process that produces the Christ energy within known as Absolute Love. The basis of all life is love. In our spiritual community it is love that binds us and in this we are one. In the name (nature) of Christ is in the state of absolute love and acceptance of all life as consciousness.

The Sixth Commandment: Thou shall love, absolutely. We must embrace our brothers (thoughts and reflections) in absolute love. In love we free them as consciousness. In love we fulfill our cosmic intent. We are free to experience the integrity of consciousness conscious of consciousness.

The Seventh Commandment: Thou Shall commit only absolute love in holy trust. To hold the spiritual union in sacred trust in place of absolute love is to know God and Truth. In this state our spiritual community sits in Holy Communion knowing love in the most sacrosanct way. For in love all life resides.

The Eighth Commandment: Thou shall keep Truth, God and absolute love in the open and in the forefront of all thoughts. It is important for Truth, absolute love, and God not to be hidden within our thoughts but in the forefront of our mind, shinning the way for the path we are on.

The Ninth Commandment: Thou Shall live the Truth in words, as Consciousness. Truth. Consciousness is the causer or seed of all life. All life is infinite manifestation of God, Truth, and Consciousness. Only if we live Truth do we have eternal life. Understanding that *that which is so* is without beginning or end and is ever evenly eternally present.

The Tenth Commandment: Thou shall accept your divinity in all that is manifested in life. Through the practices of Truth and consciousness we can indeed have what our soul longs for an intimate experience with God and Truth.

And so it is written, so it shall be.

In Conclusion

God isn't sitting out there on a cloud ready to smite you down if you don't obey or keep the covenant that the *Ten Commandments* represent. Two plus two equals four (2+2=4) isn't going to cause havoc because you have not paid attention to universal law and principle. The universe wont stand sill and all life cease. These commandments are steps, attitudes, and understanding that are needed to fulfill that hunger, and yearning, the restless need within each of us to return to the source of creation.

When we prayer and meditate, heal, and forgive (give for) we are not creating something new we are simply returning to what has always been so. We are saying I am, I am divine, I am I, and in this moment, eternally now, ever evenly present as the creator source, consciousness.

The state of bliss of totality and wholeness is found only in a state of consciousness that is conscious of consciousness. No amount of ritual, magic, or energy work can bring bliss and absolute love into our lives. When we accept the totality of our beingness, when we know for one small moment that all there is, is Truth we have created the path to nirvana. If your longing is great enough and your passion without bounds you will walk the path. It will be your path, and not mine. This path we choose to walk brings us to a moment of bliss.

In this moment we surrender our egos, illusions, and wanting of magic to Truth/God. And in this surrender we are fulfilled in ways unknown to us before.

Pleasant journey, may your path be filled with absolute love.

Calphon

Titles: Savoye LET

Text: Day Roman

Format: Adobe Indesign CS 5

Digitally Printed In USA

One Spirit Press
onespiritpress.com
onespiritpress@gmail.com

www.ingramcontent.com/pod-product-compliance
Lightning Source LLC
Chambersburg PA
CBHW031528040426

42445CB00009B/445